A personal self-love guide

I AM LOVE

Learn to love yourself and tap into your power

BY SIEDAH JOHNSON

ISBN: 9781080570119

Imprint: Independently published

Copyright © 2019 by Siedah Johnson

All rights reserved. No part of this publication may be reproduced, distributed, or transmitted in any form or by any means, including photocopying, recording, or other electronic or mechanical methods, without the prior written permission of the publisher, except in the case of brief quotations embodied in critical reviews and certain other noncommercial uses permitted by copyright law.

Table of Contents

Acknowledgments v
Introduction 1
Chapter 1: Dump It Out 9
Chapter 2: Who Are You? 19
Chapter 3: Finding Your Purpose 33
Chapter 4: Create Healthy Habits 43
Chapter 5: How Do You Want To Feel? 53
Chapter 6: Take Responsibility For Your Life 61
Chapter 7: You Are Love 71
Chapter 8: Be The Change You Seek 79
Chapter 9: Write A Love Letter 87
Epilogue: Adversity 93
About Siedah Johnson 97
About I Am Love Blog 99
About I Am Love Podcast 100
About Self-love and Personal Growth Community 101
Book reviews: 102

Acknowledgments

To god, universe, my ancestors, and guides for guiding me to get through a dark time in my life. I know I am never alone.

To my daughter, Paige Zoe Lanier, thank you for reminding mommy of the strength and power I have within. Thank you for showing mommy unconditional love. You came at a time when I had forgot what true love was. Everything I do is for you. Thank you babygirl!

To my family and friends for their support and kindness.

Special thank you to my editors and designers for your talent and kindness.

Introduction

You are a Masterpiece. Yeah, really. You are a perfect, complete Masterpiece, ready to take on the world. You are meant to live a great life, achieve your goals, have unique experiences and meet great people.

When you came onto this planet you were a bundle of joy, a bright-eyed creature just living in the moment. When you looked around, everything just... was. You had no opinions about anything. A thing was a thing, that's it. Nothing was scary, sticky, worrying or irritating, as far as you were concerned. If something came near your mouth, it went in. If something came near your hand, it was grabbed. You were a human being - just being human.

But as you explored the world, and became bigger and taller, you received messages from the people around you. Everything from how to open a door to how to present yourself. You began absorbing these messages from the moment you could take them in. You were fed a million beliefs, all which had nothing to do with you, or the nature of reality.

The main source of this information was your family. Society was another big contributor. When your parents were raising you, they passed on the beliefs they learned from their parents in an effort to educate and protect you. Your parents learned these beliefs from their parents, who learned them from their parents... and so it goes on.

The trouble is, many of these beliefs have no roots in reality, and aren't updated for this age of information overload, global connectedness, and continuous learning. They keep us unhappy, hold us back from success and create self-loathing.

It's time we change them!

Your purpose in life is to be happy, love yourself and live without limits, taking whatever the world throws at you and molding it to something that contributes to this world. And in this journey, you'll have to make many choices, but the most important one will be choosing a destination.

There are two types of travelers in the journey of life: those who have a destination in mind and those who don't. Most don't, and without a destination in mind, they inevitably just drift around without any direction, wasting their life away and never achieving anything. They are never truly happy. They just go where their instincts take them, living so cautiously they might never have lived at all.

Why do you think they don't decide on a destination? Certainly, they must know a place where they really want to go? Well, the answer is simple – they're afraid. They fear failure. They fear the judgement and criticism of others. Because of the judgement and criticism of others they will avoid their dreams all together. But by avoiding failure like this, they fail by default.

Then there's the second, more adventurous choice: having a destination in mind. These people know they might experience failure to some degree but still, persist. Despite rejection from others, they unapologetically keep going forward toward their destination. Hope and anguish can coexist within them and still create something truly beautiful.

This is the choice that tears us apart every single day until we do something about it.

You've been in this place before (everyone has), and most of you have chosen safety, the first option. But the safest path isn't always the best path. We want to keep our attention on what matters, to listen to the call of our hearts and let the rest go. We have the best intentions, but it isn't always easy. The idea of failure grips us at our most vulnerable internal place – our inner sense of self-love. Intuitively, we know that by reaching high we are guaranteed some degree of failure when we fall short, but that knowledge offers little or no consolation. Despite setting big goals and achieving them, we are mostly unhappy. Even if we manage to satisfy our inner images of what our life should be like, after two minutes of glory we feel bored and want to pursue something else. The human mind, with its primal instincts, will take only a few minutes to come up with a "But what if…"

Setting big goals creates pressure. You create inner pressure because you want to achieve your goal, and you face outer pressure from others. Being under a lot of pressure will negatively affect your health. Feelings of anxiety, sleep difficulties, a compromised immune system, and unexplained aches and pains are common symptoms of being overly stressed out. Always wanting more can also lead to a very unsatisfying life.

Now focus, for a moment, on the purpose for which you are reading this book. Bring it to the forefront of your mind, make it bigger and brighter. Less than 10% of people go further than the Introduction in a self-help book, and even fewer people apply and implement what they read: reading isn't enough, you also have to take action.

If you really, wholeheartedly want to use the lessons in this book and change your life, you need to take responsibility. You can't use any of the equations or formulas here without taking complete responsibility for your life. Everything in this book I have done for myself by personally coaching myself through my deep depression, social anxiety, and low self-esteem.

So take it slow, but be aware, observe, and change how you behave. What you think, what you say, how you walk. All your actions have to be one with your goals. If you want to be rich, you must think rich thoughts. You can't worry about paying the bills and make a lot of money. You need the right mindset. This applies to everything, and that includes growing and nurturing love within yourself.

Many people will fall on the wayside, despite claiming they want to change, but because they never take the first step, they never actually change. They desire to change a lot, but they don't start. One of the paradoxes of human life is that the first thing we have to do is probably the last thing we want to do. But, remember this, when you start and gain momentum, nothing can stop you.

If you have questions like:

> "I am unhappy about the way my body looks. How can I change this?"
>
> "How do I overcome low self-esteem and start to feel good about myself?"
>
> "How can I stop feeling like I am inadequate?"
>
> "I've convinced myself that I am stupid. How do I overcome this?"

Then this book is perfect for you, it will teach you how you can change your inner world using the most powerful (and awesome) thing in existence: *love*.

Don't just read this book. Feel it. Feel the love. Let all the negative feelings go away. You will be in a balanced place within yourself. You won't feel low anymore, wanting to lock yourself away from the world. You will feel worthy. But your mind, with its primal instincts, won't be able to easily digest many of the things we'll talk about, but your heart will.

Go with your heart. Your mind will feel neglected and will let you know, but you'll have to control it, watch it. Letting yourself be pulled by the call of your heart, the important things in life don't always feel like the safest. Uneasiness and doubt often shroud the way. And fear has a very loud voice, but you are made for this journey.

You can't see the path ahead because you haven't yet begun. But you can see what's right in front of you now. Take the little steps we're going to discuss every day; you can make the whole journey by just looking at what's in front of you at this moment in time. And however hard it seems right now, the more you persist the greater your chance of success becomes.

The dreams I had prior to going through my self-love journey were not of my own making. They were influenced by the dream my mother had for me and what society deemed successful. I adapted these dreams like my own somewhere down the line, but once I signed up for college classes or I said "I do" I wasn't happy. I wasn't happy because it wasn't my personal dream. Once I stripped away the dreams of others I found peace and joy because I was experiencing my very own personal dream.

In life, no matter how much external success we achieve, even if we become millionaires and own many supercars and live in huge mansions, we will not be happy unless we also work internally, accessing our inner power, taking hold of our feelings, getting clear on our identity and finding love within. Our riches will feel worthless and despicable without doing the inner work.

If you want true happiness, abundance, prosperity, and peace, know that it starts and ends with you. I totally understand where you are because I was there too. I was afraid of using my voice and standing up for myself. I doubted my self-worth. It is a horrible and depressing feeling when you don't feel good about being yourself. Everyone around you can tell you how beautiful you are, how smart you are, and that you're successful, but if you don't believe it then you will always feel like you lack.

I wasn't truly happy with myself, my marriage, or my life. I sat there and waited for someone to pick me up and make my life okay. Eventually, I realized that the main person I needed was myself. I picked myself up. I was sick and tired of being sad all the time.

"Sad" sounds very childish, like something flimsy, something one should be able to cast off with a happy reflection or the smile of a friend. But "sad" is nothing of the sort. Sadness sits inside, the germ seed of self-hate and depression, just waiting for the right conditions to grow, to send out roots to choke the hope out of your heart. You are down in the trough and struggle to return to the peak, always afraid of falling flat on your face. I've learned some priceless lessons like knowing that happiness is a choice, and that acceptance is a gift. I'd rather look for the lesson during troubling times than continue to focus on what went wrong because I was able to let go of the pain when I focused on the lessons learned. I believe the lessons we learn are the silver lining and make us wiser.

Introduction

In life, we can make decisions for our life so we can navigate where we're going in life and how we want to feel. Or we can let life happen to us - not really knowing where we're going or what we're meant to do. When you make a choice in where you want to go, who you want to be, and how you want to feel, you have more clarity and direction.

In this book, I am going to take you on a journey towards self-love. There's this stigma about self-love that we are being selfish when we show ourselves love. To me, self-love is about creating healthy and loving communication, habits and boundaries with oneself and others. These are practices and lessons I've personally experienced and have distilled those lessons that I learned in that dark time of my life.

Let the journey begin.

I Am Love

Chapter 1
Dump It Out

I remember the year of 2013 so vividly. I was sitting on the living room couch crying my eyes out, with the volume on the television turned up so I wouldn't wake my ex-husband who laid sound asleep upstairs. I constantly felt like I was alone. When I had enough time to reflect on my life I would sit and sob for hours at a time.

I didn't know at the time that I was in a deep depression. I was supposed to be happy according to everyone else. I was depressed because I was living a life that wasn't authentic. Loss, whether loss of a loved one, a relationship, a job, or any other loss, and constant change can be difficult to deal with in any capacity.

I've come to an understanding during my journey that in order to heal you can't avoid discomfort. Not to say I have ever gotten comfortable with experiencing discomfort. However, I am no longer afraid of emotions or having to make the difficult decisions that will set me on the path towards happiness.

Throughout my life, I would write down my thoughts and the intense emotions I would be experiencing at a particular time. I didn't always feel safe sharing my emotions with others, and not everyone around me truly understood what I was feeling. My mother is an Earth sign, and she is not very in touch with her emotions. So raising a Scorpio (myself) and a Pisces (my sister) was difficult for my mother at times.

When hugely devastating things happen to us, like losing someone we love, we somehow pick up the pieces or detach from the situation altogether.

That is why it is so important to heal and grieve instead of suppressing or ignoring how you feel. Self-awareness is a key component of the healing process.

The problem with the "BIG" things is that there is both external and internal pressure connected to these kinds of grand achievements. Being under a lot of pressure will negatively affect your health. Feelings of anxiety, sleep difficulties, a compromised immune system, and unexplained aches and pains are common symptoms of being overly stressed out. Always wanting more can also lead to a very unsatisfying life. After achieving a goal people temporarily feel happy. But then they want to achieve the next thing, and so on, and so they are never satisfied. While goals and dreams are certainly beneficial, an insatiable desire to have more can leave you feeling like you are less than.

Constantly striving to get further will cause you to feel as though you are falling behind. This type of mindset comes from a place of lack and takes the focus off what you already have or have achieved. However, a grateful heart will allow you to see the good in what is currently going on in your life. The ability to appreciate the small things can upgrade your life in a big way. There is a reason to celebrate and be grateful every day with just a slight shift in perspective.

One amazing way to engrave this principle is to have a daily journal-writing habit. Writing is exceptionally helpful for those who deal with low self-esteem, depression, or anxiety. Writing gives you the opportunity to reflect and express yourself fully without any interruptions. Writing in a journal is a great way to just get it all out of your head and right before your eyes. We usually know exactly what we want in life. But most of us can't seem to get there. We have all these goals:

- I'm going to lose weight and get healthy.
- I'm going to write that book.
- I'm going to spend more time with my loved ones.
- I'm going to start a successful business.
- I'm going to learn a new language.
- I'm going to be more present and happier.
- I'm going to get my finances in order.

But here's the problem: Doing these is really hard. And it gets harder every day. Some days, it seems more realistic to just give up entirely. The whole "taking one step forward and two steps backward" pattern is getting old.

When there's a gap between who you are and who you intend to be, you are incongruent and unhappy. You're torn, mentally exhausted, and regretful. You always feel like a fraud to yourself, and probably to the people around you.

Gandhi once said, "Happiness is when what you think, what you say, and what you do are in harmony."

To be able to love yourself, the distance between the dreams you had for your life and the reality has to be as little as possible. But the thing is, if you try to tackle everything wrong in your life, you'll quickly burn out and quit. It's happened many times before. But by focusing on improvement, you also keep thinking about your past, and that leads to self-hate and ultimately, defeat to old habits. So, what's the solution? Setting a keystone habit.

A keystone habit is a habit that, once acquired, everything in your life can change. Keystone habits spark a chain reaction of other good habits and can rapidly alter every aspect of your life. There are many keystone habits, but one that has always worked for me is writing a journal. It is the most potent and powerful keystone habit you can acquire. If done correctly, you will show up better in every area of your life—every area! Without question, journaling has by far been the number one factor to everything I've done well in my life.

Here are 9 benefits of writing in your journal:

- Reduce stress
- Clarify your thoughts and feelings
- Know yourself better
- Solve problems more effectively
- Resolve disagreements with others
- Evaluate your thoughts, emotions, and behaviors from a new perspective
- Align your emotions and motivations with your deepest values
- See other people's perspectives alongside your own
- Take a definite course in action
- Explore your deepest desires

Your thoughts are powerful. Think of your conscious mind as a gardener, and the subconscious mind as the bed of soil. Your conscious mind, the gardener, is the reasoning mind. It chooses. It can choose what it watches on the Internet, what it thinks, what it spends its time doing, either playing games or reading books, and it chooses how it behaves with other people. These are the "seeds" that are planted in the subconscious mind.

It accepts what is given to it and what is believed by the conscious mind. It does not argue, and it has no reasoning capability. Whatever seeds your conscious gardener plants, these are exactly what will grow in the garden. If you think a positive thought at this moment, for example, "I am very rich and happy!" it won't be immediately translated into reality, but it will be planted in the soil, and if you water it every day and believe in it, slowly the roots will start forming and one day the plant will sprout out, and then your thought will become true. On the other hand, if you think "I am very sad and poor!" then that thought will be transmuted into reality sooner or later too.

Happy and successful people, evidently, all have one thing in common: they know how to harness the power of their minds. Depressed and self-loathing people aren't in control of their thoughts, and as you can imagine, weeds start growing in their minds, and negativity comes into their lives.

When I was depressed I was awake and walking through life taking care of my home, my then-husband, and working. I was functioning as a normal human being. Or so I thought. I had constant thoughts and habits that were unhealthy. I had unhealthy patterns that left me stuck, my emotions unbalanced, and my inner world in chaos.

Most people live their lives on other people's terms. Their days are spent achieving other people's goals and submitting to other people's agendas. Their lives have not been consciously organized in such a way that they command every waking, and sleeping, moment of their life. Instead, they relentlessly react at every chance they get. For example, most people wake up and immediately check their phone or email. In spare seconds, we hop on Facebook and check the newsfeed. We've become addicted to input. Or in other words, we've become addicted to reactively being guided by other people's agendas.

Right after waking up, I write in my journal for 30 minutes. Because I know the power of my thoughts, I know that while I have been sleeping, my subconscious mind has been brewing, scheming, problem-solving, and learning. So when I wake up, I rush to a quiet place and engage in a burst of intellectual and creative flow.

Let's begin by allowing ourselves to purge and release all these thoughts, problems, and events we're currently experiencing in our life right now. Take a moment and write down your thoughts, feelings and emotions you're experiencing.

Activity

Now let's do a simple exercise:

Find a quiet space, close your door, turn off your cell phone, or mute your notifications.

This lesson will take you 30 minutes to an hour to reflect.

- How do you want to feel?
- What are your short-term goals?
- What are your long-term goals?
- What relationships benefit you?
- What relationships hinder you?
- What changes do you need to make to reach your goals?

Write about your thoughts, your dreams, your goals, where you've been and where you want to go.

Notes:

Notes:

Notes:

"Allow your light to shine on all the mysteries and secrets hidden within you."

Chapter 2
Who Are You?

So, who are you? Do you accept who you are, and love yourself for it?

Everybody has a weakness, nobody is perfect, that's a law. Every single one of us has weaknesses and strengths which make us unique and beautiful, and there are no exceptions. There is strength in accepting your weaknesses, rather than hiding them.

If we do not accept our weaknesses, they overpower us, but if we accept them, then we can change or improve them. When we are a constant state of reaching for perfection we are living in a dreamland. We need to accept not only ourselves, but also others, for who we are and where we are in the present moment. Authenticity is when we know we are enough and we fully accept ourselves.

There's an ancient Indian tale illustrates the importance of accepting weakness. Every morning a servant of a rich man in a village would carry two pots of water tied at either end of a pole resting on his shoulder. One pot was strong and perfect, the other was cracked. By the time he reached his master's house, the perfect pot would still be full, but the cracked pot would be half empty, having leaked water along the way. This went on for a while. Every morning, the water bearer would reach his master's house with one and a half pots of water. The perfect pot felt proud of its accomplishment, of doing what was expected of him. The cracked pot felt bad, guilty of letting down the poor water bearer and delivering only half the water.

The next day, the cracked pot saw the bed of flowers along the path, streaks of sunlight dancing on their petals from a big tree above them filtering the sun through its leaves. He liked them, but they didn't do a great job of cheering him, because as they went near the master's house, he realized he was yet again only half full.

"Come on now. Add two plus two. I noticed your crack when I first bought you from the market and took advantage of it. I planted the flower seeds on your side of the path, and you watered them every day. It's because of you those beautiful flowers exist!"

It's our flaws, the cracks in our body and the scars on our skin, that let the light into our souls. We can complain and cry about these cracks and scars, or we can use them to give us strength.

One of the most powerful ways to turn any disability into a strength is to accept it and love yourself. Here are three steps to do exactly that:

Step 1: Raise Your Inner Standards

The quality of your life is the reflection of your standards. You could make millions and still stay poor in your mind. No matter how luxurious your life is on the outside, if you have no inner wealth, then you stay poor.

What's inner wealth? Self-love and peace. If you raise the standard of your mindset, you will not be shattered by failures or setbacks. You will see obstacles as an opportunity to learn and grow. You will feel inspired instead of getting jealous. You will participate in healthy competition instead of comparing yourself to others. Identify where your standards are lacking and commit to raising the bar. Think about the cost and consequences of not raising your standards.

Change your limiting beliefs and take action to silence self-doubt. No more "should do" and way more "I must do." No more "I can't" and way more "I will." If you want to change in your life, you must be committed to changing. Most people quit on themselves. They don't stick with what it is they desire for themselves when they start to face resistance or challenges.

This is a practice that will be implemented each time you're approached with limiting beliefs or asked to lower your standards. It is then when you must make a choice: be brave and stick to your guns or fold and give up.

Step 2: Be Grateful

These days almost everyone wants to get ahead. No matter how far they have come, they want to go farther. Nothing is enough. This type of mindset focuses on lack, what you don't have, instead of what you do have. Notice what you have, and be grateful. A grateful heart will allow you to see the good in what is currently going on in your life. The ability to appreciate the small things can upgrade your life in a big way. There is a reason to celebrate and be grateful every day with just a slight shift in perspective. You can use your journal, that you started in Chapter 1, to write down what you are grateful for every day.

Trust me, gratitude can make a huge difference. Saying what you're grateful for simply shifts your energy and mindset into a higher vibration, which then leads to joy, happiness, and appreciation.

Let's dive a little deeper into what gratitude is exactly.

Gratitude is the quality of being thankful and the readiness to show appreciation for and to return the kindness. I practice gratitude every morning and whenever I feel low. There was a trigger switch within me when I focused on what I was grateful for versus what was wrong within me and around me. Gratitude reinforces moral behavior.

One of the easiest ways to be more joyful is to notice little pieces of joy life throws at us every day. Even on our bad days, if we look closely we made progress and were given great gifts by life which we didn't notice. You have to look for the everyday joy like this by yourself.

Unfortunately, your habits and mindset are against this. Our brains are wired in such a way that we can never appreciate something for a long time. So, once we get something, no matter how valuable it is to us, after a couple of minutes we want something else. Being happy with what we already have is not normal for us, we always want more. Be grateful for where you are and what you currently have.

It is exceptionally special when another person goes out of their way for you. Appreciating others means appreciating yourself. You get what you give others, if you give love, you get love; if you give happiness, you get happiness. In a similar way, if you give hateful thoughts, you will get hate, not necessarily from the same person, but in some way or another: there's no way out. This is a fact that is responsible for almost everything in our life, yet most of us are blind of it. But as important as this is, don't let this be limited to others, also appreciate yourself and be happy with yourself. Being nice to others, but giving yourself hate, will not lead to happiness. Your mind, your body and you yourself work very hard, and a little gratitude can go a long way.

Step 3: Adopt a Positive Mantra or Affirmation

"Loving or hating the life you are living is solely all in your repeated self-talk."
-Edmond Mbiaka

Repeating positive statements or declarations, also called affirmations, is a self-talk technique for changing your attitude and developing positive habits. Affirmations are an effective technique for self-improvement, and for improving your life because they imprint your intentions and desires on your subconscious mind. Pay attention to what is going on in your mind, and you will discover that your mind is a constant state of thinking. There is a constant self-talk activity going on. You can use this self-talk to your advantage when you know how.

Constant repetition is the secret key. Repeating positive words and statements will guide your mind in the right direction and push out the negative thoughts.

Repeating affirmations is a powerful mental programming technique, which is not appreciated enough and is not well understood. To affirm means to "make firm," which means making your desire or goal firm or real. It is a process of making positive statements about your goal. A statement that is often repeated affects the subconscious mind, which then uses its enormous power to find ways to make it come true.

Your affirmations will become self-fulfilling prophecies after a while if you believe in them. According to Dr. Mona L. Schulz, a leading neuropsychiatrist, repeating affirmations physically changes the neural pathways in your brain. Those changes in the neural pathway lead to changes in action that are consistent with your new belief. Affirmations are a highly effective way to reprogram your subconscious mind. Examples of affirmations are "I shall use my talents, gifts, and abilities to create wealth" or "I am living a life of purpose and wealth."

Here are some guidelines for your affirmations:

1. Always phrase your affirmations in the present tense. You want to achieve your goal now, not in some indefinable future. For example, if your goal is to find a job, don't say, "I will have a job," using the future tense. Say, "I have a well-paying and wonderful job, which I love and enjoy".
2. Use only positive and constructive words, describing what you really want to attain or achieve.
3. Be specific. Tell your mind exactly what it is that you want.
4. Keep your affirmation short and easy to remember.
5. You should also include feelings and strong desire. You should feel and believe that what you are saying is already true. Feelings and emotions give life to your words.
6. You may repeat affirmations at any time you want or at special set times during the day. Immediately after waking up and before falling asleep are two very appropriate times, as at these times it is easier to get to the subconscious mind.
7. You may repeat affirmations aloud, mentally, or by writing them down.

The thing is, as a species, humans have many differences. Race, culture, location, and circumstance all ensure that we each have our own unique characteristics and no one person is the same. But there is one thing in common with all of humanity: our propensity to talk to ourselves. We chatter away to ourselves constantly and often may not even know we're doing it. While we may not pay much conscious attention to our self-talk, it plays a huge role in our emotions, behaviors, and actions.

As such, actively acknowledging and directing your self-talk is a vital step in achieving happiness, success and everything you want in life. For example, each time you fail at something, you might say to yourself something along the lines of, "That's okay, I'll try better next time," or "I'm useless at this, I should just give up now." Whether you choose to think or speak positively (the first example) or negatively (the second) to yourself influences your choice to get back up and try again or wallow in self-pity and never seek to achieve anything of note with your life.

Entrepreneurs, for example, are well-known for their seemingly endless positivity and ability to keep trying in the face of adversity. Their secret to steadfastly striving to achieve their dreams is self-talk. They're aware that beating yourself up about failures and talking down your abilities can physically manifest themselves in your consciousness and actions. You don't have to be an entrepreneur to adapt this mindset.

During the day when you're working or doing other things like reading and talking to others, your mind functions on the principle that its contents must be true, so your thoughts tend to repeat over and over in a cyclical fashion with regards to a particular experience or issue you've faced or are about to face. When this happens, take note of these thoughts and just observe them. There is no need to address them at this point — just acknowledging them and being aware of their contents is an important step.

When you say affirmations and monitor your thoughts for some time, you can try changing your self-talk. Take what your mind is thinking and consciously turn it on its head.

According to "What to Say When You Talk to Yourself," by Shad Helmstetter, we spend more time talking to ourselves than any other person on a daily basis. The things which we tell ourselves determine our mood, decisions, and attitude and, yes, we are highly likely to believe the things which we tell ourselves. By taking control of your self-talk, you can start to live your life according to the way you want it. Your subconscious mind can believe this self-talk and begin to manifest the things which you tell it. As such, right after your affirmations spend some time every day making positive self-talk about the things which you desire in your life. By repeating this every single day, you are guaranteed to start creating a new positive reality for yourself.

For example, have you ever had a day where it seems every interaction and situation you encounter is negative?

Perhaps you woke up, looked outside your window and saw it was raining, and thought to yourself, "Well, today is going to be a crummy day."

Your subconscious mind will then take this directive that today will be a "crummy" day and see to it that everything you do and attract into your day will align with that thought. That's why it's so important to use affirmations that are positive and align only with the outcomes you want to invite into your life. If you want positive outcomes, then doesn't it make sense to input positive commands into your subconscious?

Let's take another great example: telling jokes. You tell a joke you thought was funny to a group of friends and none of them laugh. Awkwardness ensues, and you begin to tell yourself that you're obviously not a funny person and you should quit trying to be a comedian. Stop this thought in its tracks and instead say to yourself something like, "I'm hilarious. Maybe they just didn't quite understand the punchline." The act of saying this to yourself helps to convince your subconscious mind that you are indeed funny, and the next time you tell a joke you'll be surprised to find that people think you're funny, too. Because the trick to telling a good joke is being convinced that your joke is hilarious. If you're laughing as you tell the joke and are clearly convinced that it's funny, other people will think it's funny as well.

One thing to remember when saying affirmations is that the subconscious mind doesn't understand words at all, so if you think you're talking to yourself like a crazy guy when you're saying them, you probably are! The subconscious mind doesn't understand words, it understands emotions. So if you say your affirmations with no feeling behind them, then you will see no results. If you want to develop happiness in your life and say, "I am a happy person," but say it very blandly, then you won't see any change, because your subconscious mind won't be able to pick it up. Say your affirmations with great emotion. No need to be pretentious, but just try to be a little more powerful, then you will see real change.

By writing and saying affirmations, you literally become the author of your own life, and your story, so what do you want the next page to say?

Here are a few examples for the affirmations you might want to use:

- I am love.
- I approve of myself.
- I love myself deeply and fully.
- I am worthy of joy and love.
- My life is a gift. I will use this gift with confidence, joy, and exuberance.

I will surround myself with positive people who will help bring the best out in me.

Activity

Now let's do a simple exercise:

Create your own mantras that would benefit you in the present moment or future.

When you create your mantra remember to speak it into existence. Instead of "I want to be abundant." say "I am abundant."

Write down the things you are grateful for to keep a record of them daily.

This exercise will help you to eventually shift your mindset from negative to compassionate.

Notes:

Notes:

Notes:

"I am love.
I am all things.
Everything is me".

Chapter 3
Finding Your Purpose

What is your purpose? Is it some woo-woo thing that only people who meditate and chant in a cave get? Is it some religious term for holy saints? What exactly is it? Beyond religious connotations, a purpose is simply your life's message. It is the message you wish to drive in the world during your time on Earth.

An example of a life purpose is "To inspire everyone to greatness" or "To make sure no children go hungry" or "To promote health and fitness" or even "to get rich and famous." Or mine: bringing out untapped human potential.

Having a purpose can give us energy and applying it our lives can improve it tenfold. And you don't have to have a big purpose that applies to your whole life too, your purpose can change every few days, and you can have different purposes for every department of your life, like your career, your relationships, your finances, and your health and fitness.

You can use the power of purpose to get to the root of your problems *or* to get rid of them. So, in the context of this book, you can ask yourself, "What is the root of my feeling of not being enough?" or "Why do I feel unmotivated most of the time? What's the root of my problems? Where does it originate from?" or "Why don't I feel the way I want to feel? What's holding me back?"

A lot of successful people avoid complacency and mediocrity by having a positive purpose, and by answering the Why question. Why do you get up in the morning? Why do you go to work? Why do you go to the gym? Why do you eat healthily? By answering your Why in any part of your life, you motivate yourself and give yourself more energy.

Now, what I want you to understand is the importance of momentum, and more importantly, improving daily by 1%.

In this era of the "Microwave" generation, with instant coffee, fast food, get-rich-quick schemes, and lose-weight-quicker regimens, we all need to learn from the Chinese Bamboo.

Moving forward in life is a lot like growing and nurturing a Bamboo tree. It takes a Bamboo tree 3 years to grow in the ground before sprouting up to the surface. A gardener who wants to grow Bamboo trees needs to practice patience.

Without that patience two things could happen; either you won't be able to experience the beauty of the tree while it grows because you've decided to not show it anymore attention and it will eventually die from neglect.

When it came to me finding out what my purpose is was an interesting one. While in my dreams a few years ago an image of a book appeared to me. As well as the words, "Speak Up, Speak Now". At first, I thought that I needed to title by book "Speak Up, Speak Now". After spending some time pondering over that title I realized that it didn't mean that at all. Yes, I should write everything I have experienced down on paper. Also, I should speak my truth to the people as well.

I've been with a few spiritual advisors, omens, and the figure "Thoth" who also confirmed this over the years confirming that I am meant to record, share my story, and speak my truth to help others.

How do you get unstuck?

What you want can be obtained if you believe. Seriously, it is not a cliche. Would you rather steer the boat that will bring you back to shore OR allow the boat to choose the path for you?

When you're stuck between who you are, who you want to be, and who you should be and you've hit a roadblock, it can be difficult to navigate. In this article, I am going to discuss the steps you can take to get out of a rut. How to put a plan into place and how to take action on that plan. How to stay motivated when the plan isn't going the way you originally wanted it to. And finally, how to overcome the fear that keeps you stuck?

The two biggest hurdles most need to overcome that holds them back the most is fear of failure and perfectionism. However, sometimes life happens and our experiences can stunt your growth if we allow. Especially if those experiences are stressful or devastating.

If the path original chose turned out the be the path that doesn't necessarily align with your deepest desires and values then it's time to go back to the drawing board.

I invite you to create a new plan or try something new that will help you to change the course of your life.

You know never where you'll end up until you get there. And that is what makes the journey of life interesting and exciting. Decide what you want to do and then give it a try.

So no matter where you are in your life or whatever you've been experiencing lately know that you are more than capable to pull it together and start to walk down the path of your choosing.

How do you trust yourself?

We've heard it all, but how do we do it? Our intuition is the inner guide that communicates to us. Sometimes this communication can warn us and keep us from harm.

Other times, it can help us make decisions for those important and exciting decisions we need to make or even the most simple tasks. When you begin to trust yourself something magical happens. I'd like to share with you tips to help you begin to trust yourself.

I believe it is important to trust yourself because when you do you can make decisions for yourself that benefit you. When we integrate the opinions of others in our decision making it carters to them, not to us. Our intuition guides us based on our past experiences (consciously and subconsciously) and memories. Our intuition is connected to our mind, body, and spirit.

Intuition is a process that bridges the gap between the conscious and nonconscious parts of our mind, and also between instinct and reason. Following your intuition has everything to do with listening to your body. It's a subtle signal and a message follows. The more in tuned you are with your body, thoughts, and feelings the better. Everyone is different and there isn't a one of doing things.

What's best for another isn't always best for us. Therefore, I recommend that you listen to that inner voice when it first speaks to you. Better than your parents, your spouse, or society. No one knows what's best for you better than you do because you know what is going to make you happy. Even if you're not one-hundred percent sure how things will turn out. You at least know how you want to feel throughout the experience, right?

Not sure if you have had dreams like I did or you have an idea of what you are meant to do or not. You don't know unless you try. By trying something out for the first time and giving it a chance you will discover if you like it or not. Prior to writing this book and prior to I Am Love blog I was a web and graphic designer. I designed since I was 10 years old and then I fell out of love with it.

You might be destined for more than one career, more than one purpose. You won't know unless you step out on faith and see how you feel when doing it.

There is beauty figuring out your, "why?"

Why am I here?

You were born to make a mark on life and not all of us take on that challenge. A lot of us allow fear to hold us back from experiencing what life has to offer us. Our purpose doesn't always pay the big bucks. Or it can take time to make the money you may want.

> "We all have that special gift we can contribute to the world."

37

Activity

Below answer the following questions for yourself to discover the little clues leading you towards your purpose:

- What motivates you to get out of bed?
- What are you passionate about?
- What inspires you?
- What challenges you?
- What do you feel connected or in-tune with?

Notes:

Notes:

Notes:

"Old habits are not so hard to break. You just have to create better ones."

Chapter 4
Create Healthy Habits

Many people, around the new year, decide to take massive action towards their goals, but quickly lose interest and go back to their old habits. Often the problem isn't wanting to change, or even taking the first step. The hardest part is finding a way to stay motivated once our initial enthusiasm wears off or we encounter setbacks.

But imagine that instead of making mega-changes with the all-or-nothing approach to weight loss and good health, you resolve to tackle a few simple changes a day at a time. Studies show that the health and weight loss habits that have the best chance of lasting are the ones that call for minor, doable changes. This is where habits come in.

I love this quote by Octavia E. Butler:

> "First forget inspiration. Habit is more dependable. Habit will sustain you whether you're inspired or not. Habit will help you finish and polish your stories. Inspiration won't. Habit is persistence in practice."

It shows what role habits play in our life. There are days on which we don't feel like taking action. But if we are successful in forming healthy habits, they can keep us going, even when we are unmotivated.

The thing is, when we first engage in a new task, our brains are working hard - processing tons of new information as we find our way. But, as soon as we understand how a task works, the behavior starts becoming automatic and the mental activity required to do the task decreases. There are a million things that we do every day without thinking.

Brushing our teeth, drying our hair after a shower, and unlocking our phone screen so we can check our messages are all part of our routine, and they don't need a lot of brain power because they are habits. Think about how much brain power and concentration you had to use the first time you parallel parked or even the first time you tied your shoelaces. Then compare that to the amount of mental effort you exert doing those activities now. All this is because of habits.

So often we convince ourselves that change is only meaningful if there is some large, visible outcome associated with it. Whether it is losing weight and improving our health, or even building a business, traveling the world or any other goal, we often put pressure on ourselves to make some earth-shattering improvement that everyone will talk about. Meanwhile, improving by just 1% isn't notable (and sometimes it isn't even noticeable). But it can be just as meaningful, especially in the long run.

The little improvements we make every day add up to big change which lasts our lifetimes. In the beginning, there is basically no difference between making a choice that is 1% better or 1% worse. (In other words, it won't impact you very much today.) But as time goes on, these small improvements or declines add up and you suddenly find a very big gap between people who make slightly better decisions on a daily basis and those who don't.

How long does it take to create a new habit?

According to the 21/90 rule: it takes 21 days to create a new habit and 90 days to create a new lifestyle. If this is true, there are two things you need to be aware that you need most of all; one being persistence and the other being consistency.

You are going to face challenges, whether that is in losing weight, gaining confidence, or being a better partner to your spouse. In order to stop the old habits and create new ones you must persevere and be consistent with your new habits.

A muscle doesn't grow unless you are constantly in the gym. And you can't possibly reprogram your subconscious replacing those memories, habits, and communication with new data.

How do we change?

> "If you're searching for that one person that will change your life, take a look in the mirror."

This quote, in my opinion, applies for those of us who want to evoke change in our lives. Whether you want to change something within yourself or outside yourself, you're the only one who can make it happen.

I've applied these steps to changing my negative habits, core beliefs that didn't benefit me, and I let go of negative people who didn't serve my higher self.

Step one: Check in with yourself.

Think about what has been done and what it is you want to do differently. This is the time to start thinking about what it is you want or you want to become. You have to ask yourself some tough questions and really consider how you want to feel.

Ask yourself questions like, what specifically do you want to change about yourself or the circumstance you're in? What are the results you desire? How do you see yourself or your life once this change takes place?

If you don't know where you're going, you will be all over the place. So this is a time for reflection. Really sit down with yourself. Write it down in your journal what it is you desire.

Whether it is a boyfriend who can't get with the program and pull his weight in the relationship. Or you recently got laid off from your job. Or you want to quit drinking. It's easy to think or talk about what you don't want. Whatever it may be, you must make a decision on what it is you want.

Step two: take responsibility for yourself and your life.

Make a commitment to yourself that no matter what you are going to make a change for the betterment of yourself. There will come a time when you doubt yourself.

Subconsciously you will tell yourself that you aren't capable of accomplishing what it is you want. However, a change for the better means you will be required to take a risk.

You will step outside of your comfort zone to take action for a better you.

You have a choice to take responsibility for where you have been and we are you are going. No one can make change happen in your life but you. Don't be one of those people who let things or life just happen to them by chance.

This is where you step out on a limb and take responsibility for your life. Therefore, you must hold yourself accountable for following through with this decision you made.

Step three: reprogram yourself.

You must create new habits and beliefs in order for you to walk into the new you. Know that you are worthy of change. Know that now, in this present moment, is always the right time to make a change. Taking a chance in life is all about walking by faith. Believing in yourself will allow you to see the path you desire before you.

Whether you are suffering from depression or you're dealing with anxiety or have low self-esteem; you must change your mindset. 99% of our life is based on our mind (our thoughts).

Changing your mindset is what self-transformation and self-growth are all about. You have to be willing to step out on a limb and do what it takes for you to create the change in your life.

Out with the old and in with the new core beliefs, new core values, new habits, and positive self-talk. Don't allow fear or fear of failure stop you from taking the first step towards a better you or a better life. Don't allow negative self-talk or doubts keep you from moving further. Don't allow anyone around you put you down or tell you-you can't accomplish your goal.

Step four: take action.

If you want to evoke change you must take action. Change doesn't happen by just thinking about it. Create goals and start walking your new path accomplishing those goals.

There will come a time when you doubt yourself and there will be people doubt you. There will be a people who say you're not able, not capable, not good enough, it won't happen for you.

When that happens, those are the key times when you need to tell that voice inside of you or that person that it's wrong. Remind yourself and others that you're not going to quit until you are standing in the change you seek.

Stay the course by motivating yourself every day towards what you want. You talk to yourself and remind yourself every day that you're going to do this. You have to believe in yourself. You have to have faith that you're going to do this or become the type of person you desire. You know you are worthy of this change and so you need to carry that confidence.

How do we hold ourselves accountable during the process of changing?

What happens when you start to take responsibility for your life? One word comes to mind for me, **liberation**. I realized that I don't have to remain to suck in vicious cycles, be around the same people just because we have a history or their family. We all have choices. We must make the hard-decisions that make or break us and our happiness.

When you step back and think about your life and how you came to this point you will ultimately have to give the majority to all the credit to you. At one point, you chose those people or that person, that school, that career, that mindset to carry around with. It was your choices in life that brought you this far.

But you know what? You also have a choice to change your circumstances, environment, and mindset.

Some things might happen faster than others, but the great thing is that they will happen. You must be patient with yourself, tackle one thing at a time, and be persistent. Will some people be disappointed in your choices, yes? Remember that the changes you are choosing to make are to make your life better.

Once you start to validate your decisions rather than others opinions and judgments, it is in that moment that you take back your power.

Activity

In this chapter, we've discussed what is necessary to create new habits that support your goals for yourself. And the importance of reprogramming your subconscious mind in support of those new habits.

Below answer the following questions:

- What is your goal(s) for yourself?
- What habits would you like to change in order to support your goal(s)?
- What course of action will you plan to take when challenge occur? How will you get yourself back on course?

Notes:

Notes:

"When we open our eyes and acknowledge the unhealthy cycles we're in, we can choose to break them."

Chapter 5
How Do You Want To Feel?

Reality is nothing but an ocean of beliefs, thoughts, ideas, and habits. Some of these are empowering and progressive and bring joy, while others are useless and limiting, even harmful. Just as the fish who is the last to see that it's swimming in a substance called water, we are rarely aware of this.

We let the world decide how we love, get married, make money, retire and do other things. We use the benchmarks it has set for us to measure our self-worth. We don't stop and ask ourselves a simple question like, "How do I want to feel?" And if we do, we might allow what others feel and need to outweigh our own needs.

Are you successful because you are rich? Are you beautiful because you wear expensive clothes designed by some guy with an unpronounceable name from Italy? Are you no good if you don't have a college degree? Instead of answering these questions by ourselves and choosing our own worth, we let the world do the thinking and the deciding, and it always underrated us.

Everything you call "the world," "the culture," and "life" was created by people with no higher IQ than you, and you can completely change it for yourself. You can make it so that you can be happy and healthy, achieve your goals, have great relationships and be truly successful, in your own mind and not by the benchmarks set by the culture. You can decide how you want to feel: confident, sexy, intelligent, unique, rebel, etc.

Today I want you to become conscious of your daily routine and how you feel when you wake up, go to work, spend quality time with your family and friends. Become aware of what makes you feel good and happy so you can make a conscious decision to do more of that. How you feel matters. It's time for you to see the light while you are in the darkness.

You might have to make some really hard decisions in order to get to the place you desire. Not everything you do right now will help you get there, so you have to adjust and change. You may be around people who make you feel unhappy or limited, so you might have to let go of the negative people to make room for the positive. You might have to change jobs because your current job doesn't make you happy. You might want to lose weight because you're not comfortable where you are right now. You might want to leave a relationship that doesn't benefit you. You might want to step out and open your own business. You might want to travel the world.

Ask yourself, "How do I want to feel? What is it going to take in order for me to feel this feeling in a healthy and productive way?"

Whatever you focus on in your conscious mind, grows in the subconscious mind. Returning to our gardener and garden analogy from before, if you plant seeds of love, then you get more love. But on the other hand, if you plant seeds of negativity, you grow negative.

Whether you want to lose weight, gain more confidence, change careers or heal yourself from depression or anxiety you may do so by changing your focus. There is a reason why you might go to the gym for a short period of time and then quit and never reach your goal. There is a reason why you focus on trauma in your life instead of how to heal and make positive change.

For example, going into your weight loss regimen, if you keep thinking about what you have yet to do, ignoring what you have already done, then you put your mind on a level of lack, and as those thoughts of lack keep growing, that is all that you will think about, eventually eating up all your motivation to follow the regimen.

What we all have in common when dealing with depression and social anxiety is we constantly tell ourselves things and ask questions that don't benefit us. You must change how you communicate with yourself and where you place your focus. What you focus on and where you place your awareness is essential to how you view yourself, others, and the events in your life.

When you care what people think of you, you are giving them your power, your energy, and control. We have a tendency to want to be liked or accepted by others, so we spend our time guessing what others think or feel about us. This assumption we placed in our minds isn't backed by any valid facts and yet we accept it in our minds.

It doesn't much matter what others think unless you allow it to. What matters is what you think of yourself. The way you speak to yourself and think about yourself. Make it positive. Make it good. The unhappiest people on the planet are those who care far too much about what other people think. Never hand your life over to others.

Pursuing change and self-improvement can seem like a lonely road at first, and it carries the risk of alienating our friends and family. But if we feed our self-love and bravery and listen to our courageous hearts more, we learn that the "tougher" path of using our full potential and not letting ourselves be limited by others is the only path to long-lasting success and happiness.

The ones who criticize you don't know you as well as you do, they don't know your inner desires, they don't have to live with the consequences. Heck, it's not even their life so why's it their business?

The greatest miracle of your life is that you are in charge of it. People are entitled to think whatever they want, and the same applies to you, but what others think of you cannot decide your worth. You are much more than that, and at the end of the day, you are the only person who needs to approve of your own choices. If you think about it, if you follow other people's opinions, whose life are you living anyway?

So how do you stop caring about what others say and think about you?

Simple: you make a commitment to yourself to stop caring. That's it. Sounds simple as hell, but this is going to be a huge commitment. A commitment you need and deserve.

One of the fastest ways to find what is and isn't working is to look at the results you are producing. You are either healthy or unhealthy. You are either moving towards health and happiness, or away from it. And when you notice you want to change your results, take responsibility and start working on it.

Activity

Now let's do a simple exercise:

Being self-aware isn't only about the mind but about the body and the emotions as well.

Questions to ask yourself:

- How do you want to feel about yourself?
- How do you want to feel about X (kids, relationship, work, etc)?
- What do you want out of life?
- What areas in your life do you need to heal?
- What does success mean to you?
- What are your habits and behaviors helping and hindering you from being successful?
- What are your beliefs?
- What are your standards?
- What are your strengths?
- What are your weaknesses?
- Who is a part of your support system?

In the notes, write down how you feel right now and how you want to feel.

By writing this down it will make you aware of where you are and where you want to go. It will also be a point of reference if you get stuck along the way.

Notes:

Notes:

"Instead of hiding or suppressing your emotions. Allow your emotions to be felt fully in a safe space."

Chapter 6
Take Responsibility For Your Life

For true happiness, you need to take responsibility for your life. You see, one of the myths of our culture today is that we feel we are entitled to a great life. That somehow, somewhere, someone (maybe even the Universe, but certainly not us) is responsible for filling our lives with great things, great health, secure finances, and nice relationships, just because we exist.

But the truth, which you will have to accept if you want to become happier, is that there is only one person responsible for the quality of the life you live right now.

You. Yes, you.

If you want to be successful, you have to take full responsibility for what happens with you, and that includes the level of your achievements, the results you produce, the quality of your relationships, your physical state, your emotions, your income, your debt, everything!

This is hard because we've been taught by society since we were children to blame something outside of ourselves for the parts of our life we don't like. We blame our parents, our bosses, our co-workers, our friends, our organization, our media, the weather, our government, our fellow citizens, and maybe even planet Earth.

When we're unhappy, we automatically look for anyone or anything we can pin the blame on. Although these factors might be a contribution to our journey, we can't deny that the root of all our problems is ourselves.

When you are brave enough to look within yourself for your problems you reach an awesome level of freedom. Your jaw drops, realizing this simple yet fascinating fact that you've been the only person responsible for your life experience.

When you step back and think about your life and how you came to this point. At one point, you chose those people or that person, that school, that career, that mindset to carry around with. It was your choices in life that brought you this far. But you know what? You also have a choice to change your circumstances, environment, and mindset.

Some things might happen faster than others, but the great thing is that they will happen. You must be patient with yourself, tackle one thing at a time, and be persistent. Will some people be disappointed in your choices? Yes. Remember that the changes you are choosing to make are to make your life better. Once you validate your decision-making than others opinions and judgments you will start to ignore or not let them get to you.

How many times have you been faced with a situation where it totally upended your world and you wondered how could this ever be happening to you? Maybe a spouse left you, or maybe you lost business or a friend, or your health was jeopardized. Maybe it wasn't something that traumatic, but it felt like the end of the world to you. How did that make you feel? Did you want to scream at the top of your lungs? Punch a wall? Or something worse, even?

Life is 10% what happens to you and 90% how you react to it. Why? Because no matter what the situation, no matter how bad or catastrophic it might seem, if we equate our self-worth or happiness or our existence to another person, place or thing, we'll crumble on the inside.

Now, I'm not saying that you shouldn't be sad or mad if something horrible happens. However, life will continue to happen regardless of how you react to it. So why not react in a positive way? It might seem like a callous statement on the outside, but I assure you that it comes from a place of pure sincerity. Because, we all have that one friend or know that one person, who no matter what the situation, they always seem happy, right?

So why is that? Don't you think that person is ever faced with bad circumstances?

Life is not about what happens to you. It's just not. Your happiness cannot be tied to a person or a possession or even a concept. Money will not buy you happiness. Nor will another person. Your self-worth is more than that. As much as you feel that it might not be, it is. Because we've seen it throughout history.

Bad things happen to everyone, including good people. That is part of life. But the point is that you can't allow other people or situations to dictate your happiness or your self-worth or self-esteem, because life isn't about what happens to you, it's about how you react to it. And how can you react positively when your entire self-worth is tied up into that other person, place or thing?

When you feel emotions such as, sadness loss, anger, guilt, or shame, allow yourself to feel it and experience those emotions because they are real. Just don't live in that place for too long. Give it to the universe, release it into the void. We are all interconnected in this world. We all came from the same single source, no matter what you believe in. And life truly is temporary. We're here for a moment then gone the next. So live it like it's meant to be lived.

It doesn't feel good to have a bad thing happen to you. I know. Believe me. I've struggled with failure and loss for many, many years. Just as much as the next person has, if not more. But, each and every single time, I've picked myself up and pushed myself forward. I didn't let it completely decimate me to the core because if I did then I wouldn't be sitting here right now writing this book for you. All too often, we easily give up on things, and even on life as we know it, and we retreat like hermits back into our caves.

That's not the way to live. That's not what your life is meant to be. You can't allow that bad situation to deplete you, or to define you for the next stages of life. Whatever it is, other people have also struggled with it. You're not the first and you won't be the last. You're one of 7 billion souls on this planet who are going about their lives, moving from one point to the next. Sometimes bad things just happen, and they may continue to happen for the rest of your life.

To make this philosophy easier to understand and apply, let me introduce you to a simple equation:

$$E + R = O$$

(Event + Response = Outcome)

The idea behind this is that every outcome you experience in life is the result of how you responded to an earlier event of your life. If you don't like the outcomes or results you are getting right now, there are two ways to change it.

You can blame the event (E) for your lack of results (O), which is what most people do. Blame your boss, your friends, your government, everything under the sun. But remember, if they were the deciding factors, nobody would ever succeed in this world.

Remember, for every reason you can come up with rationalizing that it's not possible, there are thousands of people who have faced the same circumstances and succeeded. They overcame the barriers that their mind had created, by understanding that they are literally the only person responsible for their lives! They stop thinking limiting thoughts and are always aware of what they say. When they are about to say something limiting and negative, they instead turn it into something positive and motivational.

They choose the second option: change your responses (R) to the events (E) until you get the outcomes (O) you want.

If you complain and blame other people and things, then you need to change your thinking, your communication, your body language, that will change your behavior. That is all you really have control over anyway. Unfortunately, most of us are so run by our habits that we never change our behavior. We get stuck in this loop of conditioned responses - to our families, our co-workers, and the world at large. We are all walking bundles of conditioned responses. If you want to change and improve your life, you have to regain control over your thoughts, your images, your dreams, and your behavior.

This is the true meaning of being self-aware.

The moment you change your responses and stop blaming, your life will get better, but on the other side of the coin, if you don't do it, then you'll keep getting the same results, or even worse results. If you want to be a winner, a champion, then you need to acknowledge the truth - it is you who took the actions, thought the thoughts, and felt the feelings that got you to where you are right now.

- You are the one who took the wrong job.
- You are the one who ignored your intuition.
- You are the one who chose to be lazy.
- You are the one who abandoned your dream.
- You are the one who stayed in that relationship.
- You are the one who wasted money on unnecessary, expensive stuff.

All blaming and complaining comes from this image of something better. If you thought there wasn't a better job than yours, you wouldn't be complaining about it. If you thought there wasn't a car faster than yours, you wouldn't be complaining about how slow it is. So, if you are complaining about something, that stands proof of two things: you know something better exists, and you aren't willing to take the risks and put in the work to get it.

Take gravity, for example. Have you ever heard anyone complain about gravity? Well, I haven't. And why is that? Because we've accepted it as a natural thing. We know we can't change it, so we don't complain about it. When a dish falls on the ground and is broken into hundreds of tiny pieces, we might call ourselves clumsy, but we don't blame gravity. It's there, it can't be changed, so no use saying anything.

Instead, we use it to our advantage. Almost every sport we play uses gravity. We ski, sky-dive, high-jump, throw the discus and javelin and play basketball, baseball, and golf - all of which require gravity.

If you relate to that previous list, then by taking responsibility, you can instead:

- Learn to cook healthier food.
- Say no to peer pressure.

- Trust your own gut feelings
- Develop an action-oriented mindset.
- Learn to let go of connections that aren't beneficial to you.
- Read books and educate yourself on how you can follow your dreams.

Determine your priorities, and stop buying anything that is not on that list.

Activity

Here's an exercise you can do to help you take responsibility for your life:

Step 1: Write down the areas of your life where you feel out of control.

Step 2: Now write down what you can do in those areas of your life to feel more in control and grounded.

Example Step 1: Being a single mother I feel imbalanced, stressed, and overwhelmed with everything that I need to do.

Example Step 2: I can create a schedule that works for myself and the baby. I can ask my friends and family to for help for 1 hour or 2 hours a week when I need some "me time". I can set up playdates so my daughter and I both have some fun time with another family.

Now it's your turn...

Notes:

Notes:

"True freedom is felt when you are the creator of your life."

Chapter 7
You Are Love

It's easy to look for love outside of yourself. However, I promise you, even if you find it, that you will still feel that you lack love. Especially if people who you love disappoint you. I am here to reassure you that you do not lack due to someone or something. You show and give love because you are love. Truly it is about you believing in yourself again. You believing that you can be who you are and do anything. You have to make yourself believe or you will remain stuck in this puddle of over giving, overcompensation, and lack.

You are love.

You don't have to give and give and give to feel that. You don't have to bend and bend and bend to feel that.

You are love.

> "Each morning we are born again. What we do today is what matters most." – Buddha

Knowing that you are love, you can project that out to others. Knowing that you are love is your power. Knowing that you are love is your security blanket when life gets rough. Knowing that you are love is what keeps you cozy in the lonely nights.

You are love.

By remembering that you are love, you can maintain awareness of your emotional triggers, and take a step back and analyze them. Am I feeling this so intensely because it is something I have dealt with before? How can I communicate how I feel calmly and rationally?

Be aware of the negative self-talk you have with yourself. We get enough criticism from others in the world. The last person you need beating you up emotionally is yourself. Replace your negative self-talk with loving and inspiring self-talk.

For example, you're afraid to let go of a toxic relationship because you're afraid of being alone. And that no one else would want you. You don't feel like you're good enough for someone else.

At this point I would you to talk to your younger self. Would you tell your younger self that you're not good enough for a healthy relationship? Of course not, nor would you tell your own child this.

So speak to yourself with compassion and love. Encourage yourself to walk away from that relationship that you know deep down isn't healthy for you or the other person involved. Be brave and believe that you are good enough because you told yourself you are.

Practice self-compassion and patience. During your healing process it is important to practice compassion and patience because it isn't always a quick fix. Changing your mindset about yourself might take longer than the person next to you. Your journey is your own. Be patient with yourself and be kind.

Avoid coping mechanisms that aren't benefiting you for the long-term: food, sex, alcohol, avoidance, manipulation, drugs, etc. will only serve you short-term. If you want lasting change than you will need to raise your standards for yourself and face your problems head-on with love, care, and in a healthy manner. Coping will not make your problems go away, and you will become caught in a vicious cycle when you rely on unhealthy ways of avoiding your problems.

Don't compare yourself to others. It's easy to look at someone and see how they look and what they've obtained and want it for yourself. Be careful not to be envious of the person. When you envy another it means that you feel disconnect with yourself and feel resentful of another for their qualities, possessions, or luck. That only places you in a space of negative energy. You're putting yourself down and communicating to yourself that you aren't worthy. Instead of being envious, how about motivate yourself to obtain what it is you admire, all while being grateful for what you have now.

Accept love and kindness from others. After being let down over and over again you might automatically put your guard up. That's fine. I just want you to be aware of those who see your wall up and still show you love and kindness.

It's easy to accept the bad, but it will be a constant need to remind yourself that you deserve love and kindness. You don't deserve abuse and negativity. Be careful you don't self-sabotage your relationships because you are afraid of feeling hurt and pain again.

Remain open to receiving love, support, and kindness from others. If you're not, you might just be pushing away the very thing you want the most.

Practice acceptance and patience with yourself and others. Forgiveness takes time and it comes near the end of the healing process. You can't change the past, but you can change the future. You accept what is, let go, and move forward so that you're not allowing the past to keep you bogged down and stuck. Allow yourself as much time that you need to heal from past hurts.

Success is often built on a reflexive habit of saying "yes" to opportunities that come our way. We're hungry for any chance to prove ourselves, and when we're presented with one, we take it, even—or especially—if it seems daunting. We may also tend to say "yes" out of a fear that turning down an opportunity even once sends a message that we're not interested, and we'll stop getting additional chances in the future. But success tends to attract bigger and better opportunities.

As we succeed, a key challenge becomes prioritizing the many opportunities that present themselves. We often try to do this without saying "no" definitively—we still want to keep our options open. Inevitably, though, this results in a lack of clarity and overcommitment, and we wind up disappointing people, exhausting ourselves, or simply failing. To prevent this we need to learn to say "no" gracefully but firmly, maintaining the relationship while making it clear that this is one opportunity we're choosing not to pursue. And success in this effort is founded on the ability to manage the emotions that come up when we close a door or extinguish an option.

These emotions can be subtle: a twinge of regret, a trace of anxiety, a faint voice that whispers, "Are you sure you want to turn this down?" We often respond reflexively to such emotions, driven to eliminate the discomfort they evoke. So we say "yes" and feel some relief—until later when we realize the costs of the commitment we've now made. A critical step in managing these emotions is training ourselves to resist that initial reflexive response. Get comfortable with discomfort.

Think about it. If you have a terrible head cold, can you take care of people without feeling sluggish or weak? Can you give them 100%? No! That is exactly how it is when you have low self-esteem: you aren't 100% and you are trying to give more of yourself to others, but you only end up feeling worse.

Surround yourself with the right people and places that make you happy. Make wise decisions for yourself. Put yourself first and take care of yourself. Know your worth. Take life one day at a time. By doing these things and cutting out bad patterns you will boost your self-esteem.

Activity

Write down in one half of the circle the beliefs about yourself that were told by another. In the other half of the circle write your beliefs about yourself with no outside influences.

In the center, write similarities. Based on those similarities

What rings true to you?

Why do they?

Is it something you want to change?

Notes:

Notes:

"Stop searching for love. You are the love you so desperately seek."

Chapter 8
Be The Change You Seek

Change isn't always easy, but it is necessary. We can choose to evolve slowly, rapidly, or not at all. You have free will. You can wake up at the same time every morning and go to bed at the same time every night. There is nothing wrong with routine, especially when your routines make you happy.

If you're not happy with your life then it's time to make a change. Change is only difficult because we make it difficult. We resist change from occurring within us and in our lives. I can be very stubborn and fixed so I personally can admit that I tend to resist change when it occurs in my life from time to time. I've learned over the years that resisting change just makes your life more difficult. There were times where I could have avoided much unnecessary suffering if I just went with the flow or made that tough decision sooner.

You may have to battle with yourself to make hard decisions at times. There might come a time when you will be faced with doubt and remain stuck because you don't know what to do. Trusting yourself and listening to your intuition is extremely important, especially when change is occurring.

Step 1: Check in with yourself

Are you doubting yourself? This is the time to start thinking about what it is you want or you want to become. Ask yourself how important it is that you change. Better yet, what will you risk if you don't change? Are you doubting your ability to make decisions? I totally understand. First, remember to be patient with yourself. Rome wasn't built in a day. Secondly, set small attainable goals that you can accomplish. That way you won't overwhelm yourself.

No one knows me better than I know myself. I consult with therapists, friends, family, spouses, even tarot readers and psychics. At the end of the day, I will make the decision on what is best for me after taking into consideration others' perspectives that I trust. Ultimately, I am the one who makes the final decision on everything that serves my highest good.

Often, we don't finalize a decision because we're afraid of failing or messing up. I understand that totally and I sympathize with you. So I would recommend you first do as much research as possible and speaking to as many experts that you can before you make a final decision. And then, leap.

Yes, leap. Take a chance because you only live once. If you fall then dust yourself off and try again.

Step 2: Take responsibility for yourself and your life

Don't allow life to just happen to you. You have the willpower to make decisions for yourself and your life.

What happens when you start to take responsibility for your life? One word comes to mind for me, liberation. I realized that I don't have to remain stuck in vicious cycles or be around the same people just because we have a history or are family. We all have choices. We must make the hard decisions that make or break us and our happiness.

Make a commitment to yourself that no matter what you are going to make a change for the betterment of yourself. There will come a time when you doubt yourself. Subconsciously you will tell yourself that you aren't capable of accomplishing what it is you want. However, a change for the better means you will be required to take a risk. You will need to step outside of your comfort zone and take action towards a better you.

You have a choice to take responsibility for where you have been and we are you are going. No one can make change happen in your life but you. Don't be one of those people who let things or life just happen to them by chance. This is where you step out on a limb and take responsibility for your life. Therefore, you must hold yourself accountable for following through with this decision you made.

Step 3: Reprogram yourself

The mind is powerful. Our brain will tell us to play it safe faster than a person would. By speaking back to yourself and telling yourself that what you are doing is what is best for you although it is not familiar will be necessary from time to time.

Create new habits and beliefs in order for you to walk into the new you. Know that you are worthy of change. Know that now, in this present moment, is always the right time to make a change. Taking a chance in life is all about walking by faith. Believing in yourself will allow you to see the path you desire before you. Consistency and repetition are two major keys to physically rewire the neural paths of your brain and succeed in this process.

Whether you are suffering from depression or you're dealing with anxiety or have low self-esteem, you must change your mindset. 99%

of our life is based on our mind (our thoughts). Changing your mindset is what self-transformation and self-growth are all about. You have to be willing to step out on a limb and do what it takes for you to create the change in your life.

Out with the old and in with the new core beliefs, new core values, new habits, and positive self-talk. Don't allow fear or fear of failure stop you from taking the first step towards a better you or a better life. Don't allow negative self-talk or doubts keep you from moving further. Don't allow anyone around you, including yourself, to put you down or tell you that you can't accomplish your goal.

Learn to say no to that which doesn't serve your highest good.

Step 4: Take action

Decide what you want to do and take the first step. If you want to evoke change you must take action. Change doesn't happen by just thinking about it. Create goals and start walking your new path accomplishing those goals. There will come a time when you doubt yourself and there will be people who doubt you. There will be people who say you're not capable, not good enough, or it won't happen for you. When that happens, those are the key times when you need to tell that voice inside of you or that person that it's wrong. Remind yourself and others that you're not going to quit until you are standing in the change you seek.

Stay the course by motivating yourself every day towards what you want.

You talk to yourself and remind yourself every day that you're going to do this. You have to believe in yourself. You have to have faith that you're going to do this or become the type of person you desire. You know you are worthy of this change and so you need to carry that confidence. Don't allow fear to keep you from what you truly desire. That's easier said than done. Know that change doesn't come quickly or easily, but it will come.

Activity

In this chapter, we've discussed how to be the change you seek and how to create change in your life. Manifestation doesn't happen without intentions and action. Let's explore your deepest desires:

Answer the following questions below:

- What do you want to change in your life? And why?
- What are your fears around that change?
- What would you like to manifest? And why?
- What actions do you have to take in order to create change in your life?
- Who are the supporters in your life that you will spend more time with?
- Who are the debbie downers in your life that you will spend less time with?

Notes:

Notes:

"Clearly decide what you want. Envision all of the possibilities. Fearlessly go after what it is you desire."

Chapter 9
Write A Love Letter

No one's commitment is greater than the commitment you make to yourself. Today, I encourage you to make a commitment to yourself.

When I was going through my self-transformation, I was tired of tearing myself apart. I no longer wanted to be depressed. I wanted to be happy. I was on a quest to make change and make change happen fast. I bought myself more times than I'd like to admit. I needed a reminder of why I started this path of healing and self-discovery. I always sought commitment from others or wanted honesty and loyalty from others, but what about myself?

I wasn't always loyal to my myself or honest to myself. There were times when I lied to myself that I was happy when I was wasn't. I betrayed myself time and time again for the relationships in my life. At the end of the day, I was left empty and disappointed. Not just because someone hurt me or disappointed me, but because I went against what was right for me. Because I betrayed myself and lied to myself.

When you're looking yourself in the face you must deal with yourself with compassion, empathy, and honesty. You have to be your best friend and ultimate lover. This is a tough world and when you become an adult there is not always someone there to cuddle to protect you like mom and dad did when you were a child. There will be times when you have to be your protector, your comforter, your guide, your everything...

So below is a personal letter I wrote myself almost in the beginning of my self-love journey. You will write your own, and then you can go back and reread this love letter whenever you need to.

My Love Letter Example:

Dear Siedah,

Over the years you've been beating yourself up. You've been coming down on yourself something awful. You're not your flaws or mistakes. Internally you are your own worst enemy. You're not happy. Although, you're really great at putting on a good face in front of those who aren't close to you, don't. You're not sure what it's going to take to make you happy in this new lifestyle, but you do know how you want to feel.

- -Accept who you are as a whole. The good, the bad, and the ugly.
- -Love yourself unconditionally.
- -Don't allow fear to consume you.
- -Find your strength and confidence.

Know that you're a great human being despite your flaws. Sometimes you will intentionally disappoint those who you love in order for you to be happy. You can't keep doing what you can to make everyone else happy in order to obtain this love you wish you could provide yourself.

You will fail. You will be insecure. You will be weak at times. You will be afraid. You will be judged. You will be disappointed. You will hurt.

You have a beautiful heart and you always try to do the right thing. You have to be honest with yourself and others around you. You can't pretend or lie in order to avoid disappointing others. You must set boundaries to ensure your happiness as well. Be kind to yourself. Love who you are – the good, the bad, the ugly. Love your mistakes. Love your flaws. Love the way you learn from your mistakes.

You are love,
Siedah

Activity

Now it's your turn to write yourself a love letter. You love letter should reflect where you've been, where you are today, and where you want to be in the future. This should be a letter of commitment yourself. Write from the heart and get it all down in black and white. Later on, you can go back and reflect on your progress.

Notes:

Notes:

"There is no greater or lasting commitment than the one you have with yourself."

Epilogue: Adversity

We like the easy path. It feels amazing when we are doing things that we are already good at! It gives us confidence and makes us feel better about our abilities. Plus, we do not have to confront our own vulnerabilities and weaknesses. This is why we avoid adversity whenever we can. Facing adversity isn't fun. It puts us outside of our comfort zone and exposes our weaknesses. It makes us look bad. So, to avoid this pain, your mind will motivate you to take the quick and easy path.

This mindset only gets stronger as you age. You stop seeking out challenges, you stop trying to learn new things and you value yourself based on what others think of you. This may make you feel better in the short-term, but it will ultimately set you up for failure.

People have an extraordinary ability to rise to a challenge. Even if it looks like there's no hope far out on the horizon, we can summon the willpower to do the extraordinary. When we expose ourselves to adversity on a daily basis, we see three key benefits: we increase our willpower, we learn and grow, and we become aware of our true limitations.

In the film "Meet Joe Black," Brad Pitt plays the role of the Grim Reaper (Death) who takes over the body of an unsuspecting man in order to experience what it's like to feel human. Part of that experience includes making a deal with Bill Parrish (played by Anthony Hopkins) where he graciously gives him a few extra days to live. In return, Bill must allow him into his life so that he can experience what it's like to be human.

Towards the end of the film, Joe mentions that there are two certainties in life: Death and Taxes. I bought this up because I would like to add another element to that list: adversity. Just as death and taxes are an unavoidable part of life, so is adversity. This is just how life is, and adversity is a big part of that experience. The problem with adversity is that most people never see it in a positive light. In fact, most see adversity as a sign that the world is out to get them.

However, this couldn't be further from the truth.

When facing adversity, we choose how we react. We can choose to respond negatively, or we can respond positively and learn something out of that adversity and thus be more productive. All of us have the freedom to choose our own beliefs, thoughts and the attitude we bring to every situation we face. Nobody else can choose your reaction, only you can. We also have the freedom to choose the amount of effort and persistence we bring to every task.

Herein lies the key to a great irony of our minds.

We only value things we pay for, in money or some other form. We don't value things we got for free, essentially. Our minds, our bodies, our goals, our ambitions, our drive, our families, the opportunity our countries offer. We take it all for granted, yet they are the true wealth we possess. Without them, we're nothing. A man who knows how to grow a business can lose all his money and become still richer some years later. A man with goals can fail many times, but eventually, he'll reach his goals if he persists.

All the things we've been given for free are actually the only truly valuable things we have.

Epilogue: Adversity

With this mindset, only four things matter: how you see the adversity, how you respond to it, how you maintain your composure when facing it, the story you tell yourself and others about what's going on. It almost always comes down to the story you tell yourself. How you see your life, and ultimately your adversity, changes everything.

A man was walking down a street, humming his favorite song, when he noticed a group of workers breaking stones on the roadside. They made ear-splitting "clack-clack" sounds as they went on pounding their hammers on the stones, splitting them into smaller and smaller pieces.

The man went up to one of them and asked him what he was doing. "Are your eyes at the back of your head?" he said, wiping the sweat from his face. "What else, I'm breaking these stupid, idiot stones!"

Walking for another ten minutes, he came along a similar sight. "What are you up to?" he asked one of the men working. The man got up, broke into a bright smile and said, "I'm helping build the world's tallest cathedral! Isn't that great?"

I love to compare my problems and my adversities to the size of the Universe. We are one species among the tens of millions of species who live on one planet circling one of a couple of hundred billion stars that are located in one galaxy among hundreds of billions of galaxies, all of which are in one universe among perhaps an infinite number of universes all nestled within a grand cosmic multiverse.

Our universe is perfect. It has a certain grace and symmetry. I like to think that it is so well balanced that the fact that you have a problem also works as a sign that there is a solution. And for the possibly 200 billion suns for the 100 billion galaxies in the Universe, by the time their light travels within our eyesight, they have already burnt out and don't exist anymore, just like a spark that jumps out of the log fire burns out in due time as the energy has been expended. The light is still traveling, and yet the source of the light is no longer there.

Just think about how small and short-lived this stuff is. And out of all the "dust balls" we have been able to observe with our giant telescopes, we haven't seen one yet that has butterflies, trees, waterfalls, bugs, bridges, statues, buildings, pets and beautiful human beings like ours yet. Out of billions of them, not one has this rich beauty.

Just think about how it's such a gift to be here right now, at this moment. It won't last, our sun will burn out and our little dust ball will be sucked into the vacuum of the black hole. This is the golden jackpot that we are here now, in the billions of human years, me and you, and nobody knows for certain what will happen next.

Think about that.

About Siedah Johnson
(SI-EE-DAH) means "Happy"

Mom, self-love advocate, coffee-addict, and blogger. I've battled with depression and social anxiety on and off for 15 years of my life. In 2014, I fell back into a deep depression that I couldn't get myself out of because I was battling myself. I was afraid of using my voice and standing up for myself and my self-worth. I wasn't truly happy with myself, my marriage, or my life. I truly sat there and waited for someone to pick me up and make my life okay.

Well, I was sitting for two years. I was in such a dark place that everything in my life had to come to an end and I had to start over in a healthy way. I soon realized that I had to pick myself up and dust myself off. I made a conscious decision to stop being the victim and start creating the life I desire. It wasn't an easy road and I reached out to people to help me.

Now, here I am sharing my story with you so you can avoid having to experience as much suffering as I did. You can reach deep down inside of you, pull out that strength and start creating your life full of love and joy. You don't have to experience trauma in order to create change.

Start today!

    Facebook: @iamlovexo

    Pinterest: @iamlovexo

    Instagram: @iamloveblogxo

About I Am Love Blog

I Am Love xo, Inc. | change, heal and love yourself

- Self-love
- Self-help
- Self-discovery

Since 2012, I Am Love xo was only a blog to help me document my process while I experienced a massive amount of change in my life. Writing helped me to heal myself and share my stories with others who were experiencing the same. Now in 2019, I Am Love xo is not only a blog full of my stories but of the stories of others all over the world. A supportive community for those who are on their journey of self. A resource to help you to change, heal, and love yourself.

It is love that heals all things. Here at I Am Love xo there is a directory full of those who have been where you are sharing their stories, coaches, spiritual advisors, and psychologist. A supportive community open to all providing positive inspiration, open dialogue, and support from our peers and professionals.

About I Am Love Podcast

I Am Love podcast is based on an open discussion about self-love, spirituality, and personal growth.

This is the podcast for you if you're looking to hear about real-life situations from real people. Listen to Siedah every Monday as she covers topics like self-love, spirituality, and personal growth. After a 2-year depression, she found herself going through a spiritual awakening.

Listen at http://anchor.fm/iamlovexo

About Self-love and Personal Growth Community

Our online community is on Facebook and it is an amazing group full of support during your healing journey.

Dealing with our issues alone in our homes day after day can be very lonely. This community here to uplift you, motivate you, and empower you to keep moving forward down your path towards change. You don't have to do it alone. This community was created - just for you!

You can get unlimited support from myself and others in this new Facebook group. It will take some time to build, but I am dedicated to giving my time and sharing my story further with you by all means.

Join us over at the Self-Love and Personal Growth Facebook community at bit.ly/LoveComxo to discuss our weekly topics.

Book reviews:

Siedah helps you breathe fresh air of real life when reading her book. By engaging your imagination, she goes beyond painting the picture of what a balanced, fulfilling life is. Siedah goes ahead to take you by the hand and guide you on a journey of self-love that will empower you to live a truly magical life of wonder from intelligent choices you'd make as you go along.

~ Prosper B. Wealth, Speaker on Self-love
http://prosperbwealth.wordpress.com/

Your book is personally helping me. I've always hated myself. This idea of self-love seems weird and alien but at the same time a ray of hope for me.

~ Candy, Editor

Made in the USA
Middletown, DE
12 November 2022